Historical Association of Ireland
Life and Times Series, No. 1

Henry Grattan

JAMES KELLY

Published for the
HISTORICAL ASSOCIATION OF IRELAND
By Dundalgan Press Ltd

First published 1993

ISBN 0-85221-121-X

© James Kelly 1993

Cover design: Jarlath Hayes

Historical Association of Ireland, Dublin

Printed by Dundalgan Press, Dundalk.

FOREWORD

This series of short biographical studies published by the Historical Association of Ireland is designed to place the lives of leading historical figures against the background of new research on the problems and conditions of their times. These studies should be particularly helpful to students preparing for Leaving Certificate, G.C.E. Advanced Level and undergraduate history examinations, while at the same time appealing to the general public.

CIARAN BRADY
EUGENE J. DOYLE
Historical Association of Ireland

CONTENTS

CHRONOLOGY OF GRATTAN'S LIFE AND TIMES

1746	July: birth of Henry Grattan in Dublin.
1761	Election of his father, James, as M.P. for Dublin city.
1763–7	Student at Trinity College, Dublin.
1766	Death of his father.
1768–72	Reads law at Middle Temple, London.
1772	Called to the Irish bar.
1775	Elected M.P. for the constituency of Charlemont.
1776	Outbreak of the American War of Independence.
1779	Grattan supports non-importation campaign in support of 'free trade'.
1779–80	One of the leaders of the Patriot campaign which compels the government to concede 'free trade'.
1780	Embraces the cause of 'legislative independence'.
1782	15 Feb.: Dungannon Convention.
1782	16 April: secures unanimous parliamentary backing for his amendment in favour of legislative independence.
1782	June: voted £50,000 by house of commons.
1782–3	Loss of popularity because of stance on 'renunciation'.
1783	Oct.–Nov.: altercation with Henry Flood.
1783–4	Takes independent stand on parliamentary reform.
1785	Opposes Pitt's 'commercial arrangement'.
1787–9	Advocates tithe reform.
1788–9	Regency crisis and foundation of Irish Whig Club.
1789	Outbreak of French Revolution.
1790	Grattan elected M.P. for Dublin city for first time.
1792–3	Embraces the causes of Catholic enfranchisement and parliamentary reform.
1793	Outbreak of war between Britain and France.
1794–5	Grattan plays a central role in the Fitzwilliam administration.
1797	Withdraws from the house of commons and declines to stand for re-election.
1798	Suspected by conservative critics of complicity in the 1798 rebellion.
1800	Elected M.P. for the borough of Wicklow in a futile attempt to defeat the Act of Union.
1805	Elected to Westminster for English constituency of Malton to advocate the cause of Catholic emancipation.
1806	Elected M.P. for Dublin city.
1808	Urges royal 'veto' on appointments to Catholic hierarchy.

1

1813   Catholic relief bill defeated in the house of commons.

1820   4 June: Grattan dies in London.

1822   Publication of *Speeches of Henry Grattan* (4 vols) and *Miscellaneous works of Henry Grattan.*

1839–46   Publication of Henry Grattan jr's *Memoirs of the life and times of the Rt Hon. Henry Grattan* (5 vols).

INTRODUCTION

Henry Grattan is the only Irish historical figure to enjoy the accolade of having a phase of Irish parliamentary history named after him. It is significant, however, that the inauguration of the appellative 'Grattan's parliament' to describe the eighteen years between the winning of 'legislative independence' (1782) and the enactment of the Act of Union (1800) postdates Grattan's demise. Most contemporaries, Grattan included, would have rejected the term as infelicitous and inappropriate. It is also inaccurate; the reality of legislative independence was manifestly less than the image of it forged by the nineteenth-century constitutional nationalists who popularised the term in order to give legitimacy to their efforts to repeal the Act of Union. Certainly Grattan was the most eligible eighteenth-century politician for reification in this manner. Because of his prominent role in securing legislative independence and his trenchant opposition to the Act of the Union, his career could be identified more intimately than that of any other contemporary politician with this period of Irish parliamentary history. No less significantly, his desire, first articulated in the early 1780s, to extend the definition of the political 'nation' to include Catholics and his efforts to advance the cause of Catholic emancipation at Westminster in the early nineteenth century meant that he was more appealing to the increasingly Catholic nationalist movement of the nineteenth century than figures like Henry Flood and Lord Charlemont whose views were avowedly more sectarian. Furthermore, Grattan was a very likeable individual. He may not have possessed the sharpest political mind of his generation, but he was an engaging conversationalist, a generous host and a devoted husband and father. He was also thoroughly principled, with the result that the plethora of memoirs and reminiscences produced to meet the insatiable Victorian appetite for such matter exposed few skeletons and progressively enhanced rather than tempered his reputation.

There were skeletons to be unearthed. No politician, not least one whose political career spanned nearly half a century, whose rhetoric tended towards bombast and whose political judgment was suspect, could operate without giving some hostages to fortune. However, Grattan was very effective at covering his tracks. During his lifetime he substantially rewrote the visible record of his career—his speeches[1]—while after his death his sons, Henry and James, zealously guarded his memory. Henry junior, particularly, did more than anyone to perpetuate a positive memory of Grattan as an heroic figure by publishing a substantial five-volume 'life and times' in which he sought 'to raise in public estimation the character and the services of virtuous and independent men to show their attachment to their country and to liberty'.[2] He was remarkably successful. Though a number of biographies which take a more critical view have reached print, none have entirely supplanted this work, and the image of Grattan that survives is overwhelmingly positive.

There is, one must concede, much about Grattan's career that lends itself to an heroic interpretation. From his election to the Irish house of commons in 1775 until his death in 1820 he was prominent in virtually every major debate that concerned Irish and Anglo-Irish politics. Though aspersed by his enemies as a talentless 'demagogue', he can be portrayed more accurately as a political moderate who sought to steer a course between political extremes and whose career was propelled by a palpable dislike of oppression and injustice. Moreover, because political power, in Britain as well as Ireland, during most of his lifetime lay firmly within the grasp of individuals who believed that Grattan's goals were incompatible with their aspirations of maintaining 'Protestant ascendancy' and Ireland's continued subordination to Great Britain, he spent the bulk of his political career in opposition. It was a role to which he was naturally suited. He was at his most effective when he was at liberty to engender an emotional response in his audience; and since his oratorical style lent itself to the broad stroke rather than to the careful exposition of detail such as is demanded by government, he was most comfortable and influential when he was calling on the government from the opposition benches to respond to real and perceived grievances.

BACKGROUND AND BEGINNINGS, 1746–75

Henry Grattan was born in Dublin in July 1746. His family background, like that of many of the most distinguished figures in eighteenth-century Irish politics, was professional rather than landed. Henry's father, James, possessed a small estate in County Cavan and beneficial leases to other properties in County Westmeath and Dublin city,[3] but his main source of income and status was the law. James Grattan never achieved high legal office, but he did serve as recorder for the city of Dublin with some distinction for many years. Like many lawyers he harboured political ambitions, and following his contribution to the resolution of a long-running dispute over the composition of Dublin Corporation, he achieved his objective when he out-polled Charles Lucas, the city's leading radical, in the 1761 general election.

James Grattan was essentially an old-fashioned Whig. He defined his political *credo* according to the principles of the Whig exclusionists of the 1680s, which led him, for example, to justify the retention of the penal laws against Catholics and Dissenters as necessary 'for the security of our government'.[4] Henry, his son and heir, was ill-at-ease with his father's politics. Moreover, they did not enjoy the best of personal relations. Henry was academically inclined, but his enthusiasm for literature, when he was a student at Trinity College between 1763 and 1767, displeased the recorder, who was anxious that his son should pursue a legal career. Henry had the security of knowing that the family lands were entailed to him, but they were too small and scattered to enable him to live in any comfort. The arguments in favour of his training to pursue some lucrative line of employment became compelling when he learned that his father had not bequeathed him the family seat at Balcamp on his death in 1766. Though prone at this time to bouts of melancholic introspection—a tendency accentuated by the death in 1767 of his sister Catherine and of his mother in the following year—Grattan accepted what appeared to be his destiny and went to the Middle Temple in London to fulfil the requirements necessary for a career in the law.

Grattan spent the next four years in England. He was not really interested in the law, with the result that much of the time which he should have devoted to reading the works of jurists was spent in familiarising himself with the historical and political writings of Burnet, Hume, Clarendon and Bolingbroke. The gallery of the house of commons and the bar of the house of lords possessed an equally strong appeal, and he spent hours there listening to debates and studying the oratorical techniques of Edmund Burke and the Earl of Chatham, whom he regarded as the finest speakers in parliament.

It was during these years that Grattan's political education may be said to have taken place. Political as well as personal differences lay at the root of his alienation from his father. James Grattan was hostile to Charles Lucas's persistent attempts during the 1760s to limit the duration of Irish parliaments to seven years. Henry, by contrast, was attracted by the principles of virtue espoused by the Patriot opposition in the Irish house of commons; he supported a septennial act as a means of countering political corruption, and he was encouraged in this view by his brother-in-law, Gervaise Parker Bushe, the M.P. for Granard. Bushe's circle included Henry Flood, the most talented opposition spokesman in the Irish house of commons, Hercules Langrishe and Walter Hussey Burgh, and Grattan spent much time in their company on his visits home from England. It was from these that he learned at first hand of the efforts of Lord Townshend, the Irish lord lieutenant, to increase the power of Dublin Castle in domestic Irish politics. It was these also who alerted him to the perception of liberals throughout the English-speaking world—Britain, America and Ireland—that the British government was embarked on a campaign to undo the Glorious Revolution by increasing the power of the monarchy over parliament. When he was in England, Grattan closely followed the Wilkes affair and the developing crisis in America, and he was soon persuaded by the British Whigs' argument that George III and his ministers were embarked on a co-ordinated campaign to reanimate Stuart despotism.

Grattan's personal political hero was William Pitt, Earl of Chatham. He believed that Chatham represented all that was fine and noble in British politics, just as strongly as he came to perceive that Lord Bute and, in Ireland, Lord Townshend represented all that was base and corrupt. Indeed, he was so enamoured of Lord Chatham that he wrote a hagiographical essay on him, in which he extolled his prescience and incorruptibility, for the anti-Townshend tract *Baratariana*.

Grattan's readiness to contribute propagandist essays to the anti-Townshend campaign (one of which condemned the lord lieutenant forthrightly as the 'miserable instrument of English tyranny') underlines the extent of his politicisation in these years.[5] He had, meanwhile, qualified as a lawyer, but though he endeavoured to establish a practice after he was called to the Irish bar in the spring of 1772, he did not possess the resolution to make a successful barrister. He integrated himself in Dublin society, and was soon a *habitué* of the Society of Granby Row, a liberal political and convivial club among whose members were Lord Charlemont and a new generation of able and ambitious politicians which included Denis Daly, Barry Yelverton, John Forbes, Hussey Burgh, Gervaise Bushe and Hercules Langrishe. However, Irish politics proved less gripping than Grattan had anticipated. He attended some parliamentary debates at College Green and was impressed by Flood's 'wisdom' as well as 'eloquence',[6] but Townshend's successor, Lord Harcourt, excited little of the passion and fervour occasioned by his predecessor. Grattan had to reconcile himself to a palpable decline in the political pulse in Ireland between 1772 and 1775 as first Bushe and then Flood abandoned opposition for the fruits of government employment. Because of this and his own fitful involvement with the law, it is not surprising that the years 1773–5 are among the most poorly documented and uneventful in Grattans's life.

2

PATRIOT POLITICIAN, 1775–82

I

Access to the Irish political process in the 1770s was extremely difficult for an ambitious but necessitous young lawyer like Henry Grattan. One of the traditional means of securing a parliamentary seat was purchase, but since the price in the early 1770s ranged from £1,500 to £2,500, admission by this route was simply beyond his resources. However, fate took a hand. Following the loss at sea of the M.P. for Charlemont, Francis Caulfield, his brother Lord Charlemont offered the representation to Grattan, and he took his seat in the house of commons on 11 December 1775.

Grattan was well equipped to meet the challenge posed by political life. He was *au fait* with parliamentary procedure as a consequence of his frequent visits to the British and Irish legislatures. Moreover, he had expertly schooled himself in the art of public speaking; while his practice, before he became an M.P., of elaborating his position on matters of public moment in the 'form of a speech' meant that he was ready to throw himself into the cut-and-thrust of parliamentary debate from the moment he took his seat.[7]

It was an exciting time for a young man to enter politics. By the end of 1775 it was clear that Britain's American policy had so alienated the colonists that conflict was inevitable. Shortly before Grattan took his seat the Irish parliament had responded to the mounting crisis in America by authorising the transfer of four thousand soldiers on the Irish army establishment to assist in the war against the colonists. The parliamentary opposition had resisted the move, but though they failed to deny Dublin Castle its request, their actions raised the political temperature without as well as within parliament. Grattan was quite at ease with this; his political views were such that it was inevitable that he would take his place with the other Patriots on the opposition benches. His object was to hasten the creation of a more principled political environment in which the Patriots could achieve their larger goals of commercial and constitutional equality with Great Britain. Grattan's initial parliamentary contributions were on financial matters. The opposition accused the administration of financial profligacy because of its failure to control the current budget deficit. Grattan played a supporting role on these occasions; he tended to follow the lead provided by Barry Yelverton, Barry Barry and Hussey Burgh. However, he did not want for confidence, as he demonstrated on 19 February 1776 when he criticised Henry Flood's justification of the government's decision to embargo Irish exports to the American colonies as a 'necessary action' as 'the tyrant's plea' and denounced the embargo as illegal.[8]

Grattan's eagerness to engage administration spokesmen and his penchant for 'violent' language attracted unfavourable notice from Castle officials,[9] but it won him credit with the Patriot interest inside and outside parliament. As a result, Lord Charlemont had no hesitation renominating him to represent his borough when a general election was called in 1776. This was a landmark election, since it resulted in a palpable strengthening of the Patriot interest in the house of commons. More significantly, it hastened the emergence of two definable political 'sides' in the chamber. Occupying the government benches, supporting Dublin Castle, were the upholders of the *status quo* who aspired to keep Ireland quiet while ministers in London got on with the war in America; on the other side of the house, fulfilling the traditional opposition role, Henry Grattan and the Patriots took their places eager to take advantage of the war to advance their programme of fiscal, commercial and constitutional reform.

Grattan flourished in this confrontational atmosphere. When M.P.s reconvened in October 1777 for the regular biennial session, he was ready to resume where he had left off in the spring of 1776. Determined to exploit the administration's economic difficulties, Grattan's main focus in the first part of the 1777–8 session was the state of the county's finances. Opting to leave the weightier political matter of the impact of the embargo on Irish trade to senior members of the opposition, he repeatedly drew attention to the failure of successive administrations to balance the kingdom's budget. More provocatively, he affirmed that the reason for the administration's failure to pursue such obvious remedies as the reduction of expenditure on pensions and military contingencies was that they were prohibited from doing so by the British government—'the same English administration . . . who have corrupted the constitution, [and] who have lost the empire to Great Britain'.[10]

This line of reasoning disturbed Dublin Castle because of its manifest anti-English tone, but Castle officials had little difficulty convincing a majority of M.P.s to reject such claims. However, defeats in the division lobbies did not deflect the Patriots. Though they were an *ad hoc* alliance of like-minded individuals rather than a disciplined political party, they were sufficiently encouraged by the visible impact of their arguments and the country's mounting economic difficulties in the winter and spring of 1777–8 to intensify their campaign. Grattan was still only one of their second-rank spokesman at this stage; Barry Barry, Barry Yelverton and Denis Daly usually took the lead in debate. However, he was their most outspoken and aggressive speaker, and he made an increasingly impressive impact as the Patriots consistently outargued the Castle interest in the commons by early 1778.

Inspired by this, Grattan felt emboldened to call on M.P.s on 6 February to address the king on the state of the nation. Though ostensibly just another attempt to persuade the house to support his calls for financial retrenchment, this debate represented an important milestone in Grattan's emergence as a major figure in the house of commons. Once again, his disposition to attribute Ireland's financial difficulties to the continued subordination of its economic interests to those of Britain ensured that his motion was rejected as M.P.s succumbed to the mood of loyalty engendered by news of a Franco-American *rapprochement*, but this reversal did Grattan little harm. The refusal of the British parliament to respond to mounting Irish demands for 'free trade' by agreeing a generous relaxation in the mercantilist restrictions binding Irish commerce in the summer of 1778 ensured that his popularity grew rather than diminished. Public opinion was more radical than parliamentary opinion, and it was appalled by the grudging nature of the Westminster response. As on previous occasions, Grattan was quick to identify the public mood. In one of the last debates of the 1777–8 session his outspoken criticism of the coyness with which Irish M.P.s called for government intervention to ease Ireland's economic difficulties prompted allegations that he was seeking to foment rebellion. This was nonsense, but Grattan was in the minority once again when the matter was put to a division. However, he could take satisfaction from the fact that a growing number of M.P.s now agreed with him on the urgency of the immediate liberalisation of Irish trade.

By the end of the 1777–8 session Henry Grattan had established himself as one of the leading Patriot spokesmen in the Irish house of commons. He was unquestionably more aware than most of his colleagues of the burgeoning sense of anger in the country at the failure of parliament to ease the kingdom's economic difficulties. Part of the explanation for the administration's inactivity was the poor revenue returns, which meant there simply was not enough money in the exchequer to finance new initiatives. Indeed, Dublin Castle did not have enough funds to pay for the accoutrement of a civilian militia to aid in the defence of the country in the event of a French invasion, even though an act authorising the establishment of such a body had been ratified by the house of commons. As a consequence, Protestant gentlemen throughout the country took it upon themselves to form 'volunteer' corps which were beyond Castle control.

Like thousands of others, Grattan succumbed to the Volunteering mania that gripped Ireland in 1778–9 when rumours of a French invasion were at their most plentiful. More importantly from a political perspective, he and others in the Patriot leadership were quick to appreciate that the 'serious apprehensions' created by the Volunteers in 'both the English and Irish administrations' gave them a powerful weapon they could use to press for the trade concessions they now believed essential to relieve the hard-pressed Irish economy.[11] Grattan's personal commitment to the cause of free trade increased visibly in the summer of 1779, as is clearly apparent from his active participation in the non-importation campaign which sought to promote home consumption.

His involvement with the non-importation campaign notwithstanding, Grattan was first and foremost a parliamentarian. The problem for the Patriots, as the events of the 1777–8 session had amply demonstrated, was that they were too inchoate organisationally as well as too small numerically to secure the implementation of their programme. In an attempt to combat these

B

deficiencies, Barry Yelverton founded a political and social club of like-minded individuals commonly known as 'the Monks of the Screw' on the eve of the 1779 parliamentary session. Little is known of Grattan's involvement with this influential body, but he was a member; he was also a key figure in the series of meetings organised by a small opposition cabal which led directly to the ratification by the house of commons on 12–13 October of an address to the king calling for the concession to Ireland of the right to 'free trade'.

Henry Grattan junior has described the debate on the address to the crown of 12–13 October 1779 as 'the real commencement of Mr Grattan's [political] career'.[12] This is hardly sustainable given Grattan's activities in 1777–8, but it is certainly true that his key role in the run-up to and course of this debate signalled his formal emergence as one of the leading Patriots in the house of commons. With this triumph, moreover, the Patriot leadership had seized the political initiative, and, encouraged by their success and the concurrent collapse in the morale and discipline of the Castle interest, they inexorably increased the pressure on the administration to meet their demand for commercial concessions. Their most controversial action was to threaten imminent financial chaos by approving a six-month rather than the usual two-year money bill. But their most successful public demonstration took place on 4 November, at the annual commemoration of William of Orange's birthday, when the serried ranks of the Dublin Volunteers assembled in front of the houses of parliament with cannon, muskets and placards bearing the slogans 'SHORT MONEY BILLS: A FREE TRADE OR —, A FREE TRADE OR SPEEDY REVOLUTION'.

There was unease among some Patriots at the lengths to which individuals like Grattan were prepared to go in pursuit of 'free trade'. However, most M.P.s were sufficiently convinced of the merits of the demand to support the contention, put most forcefully by Grattan in the house of commons on 23 November, that to accede to the Castle's request to vote a full complement of taxes would undermine their strategy to secure free trade. Tactically, the opposition's plan worked perfectly. By early December the prime minister, Lord North, had concluded that it was essential to repeal the commercial restrictions binding Irish trade to secure the Anglo-Irish connection. With this in view, he piloted a series of bills through the Westminster parliament in the spring of 1780 repealing the prohibitions on the export of Irish woollens and glass and opening up the colonial trade to Irish goods. Grattan and the Patriots had won; their long-sought-after aspiration of 'free trade' was now a reality.

II

The fact that the Patriots had obliged the British government to abandon its traditional mercantilist policy with regard to Ireland was an unquestioned triumph for Grattan and the rest of the opposition leadership. However, Grattan refused to engage in any hyperbolic claims for what had been achieved. He adjudged the concessions 'adequate to the wishes and . . . to the distresses of the kingdom',[13] but with 'free trade' won, Barry Yelverton and he were determined to press on and to initiate /a campaign to liberate the Irish parliament from the constitutional bonds— particularly Poynings' Law and the Declaratory Act—that restricted its freedom to legislate. Grattan assured the Dublin Guild of Merchants in January 1780 that he would 'strain every nerve to effectuate a modification of the Law of Poynings . . . [and] to secure this country against the illegal claims of the British parliament' by moving for 'a declaration of the rights of Ireland' when parliament reassembled.[14] In addition, there were vocal calls for the enactment of an Irish mutiny bill to bring the army on the Irish establishment under full domestic control, and for the emendation of the tenure of judges from *ad bene placitum regis* to *quamdiu se bene gesserint*. This, of course, was precisely what Lord North did not want; and he directed his Irish lord lieutenant, the Earl of Buckinghamshire, to oppose every effort the Patriots made to raise constitutional points. For once, Buckinghamshire was in a position to implement his prime minister's instructions. There was agreement among many erstwhile supporters of the free trade campaign that it was inappropriate to raise constitutional points at this time, but Grattan was so eager to lay the groundwork 'for carrying . . . one great [constitutional] measure next session' that he determined to press ahead regardless.[15] On 19 April he made a powerful speech in support of his contention 'that the king's most excellent majesty, lords and commons of Ireland were the only powers competent to make laws to bind this kingdom' and that free trade was vulnerable and incomplete without political liberty.[16] However, he was outmanoeuvred by the administration, which proposed and carried an adjournment motion by 136 votes to 97.

Grattan's speech in support of his motion urging an Irish declaration of rights was commonly acknowledged as an oratorical *tour de force*. Set-piece debates of this kind were his speciality. This suited his speaking style, which tended, Henry Flood observed perceptively, towards declamation rather than debate.[17] Grattan carefully prepared all but the most casual of his parliamentary contributions, and it is this fact which accounts for the profusion of metaphor, epigram and antithesis in his speeches. He also deliberately stoked the emotions of his audience by exaggerated turns of phrase and extravagant gestures. This was the style favoured by Irish audiences, and few were as able as Grattan to awe an audience, as he demonstrated so effectively on 19 April. He did not always, as the outcome of the debate on 19 April also attests, convince a majority of his auditors to side with him; but the impact of his contribution on this and subsequent debates in the spring and summer of 1780 placed the question of legislative independence firmly at the top of the domestic political agenda. Moreover, the enthusiastic response accorded to his 'declaration of rights' motion in the country at large indicated that his fame was continuing to grow.

Grattan took heart from this approbation; but the Patriots, as a whole, were disappointed by the outcome of the session, which concluded without the administration conceding any constitutional point. Grattan consolidated his political reputation with a defiant justification of the right of the Irish parliament to act as an autonomous legislature in a pamphlet on the mutiny bill in the autumn. But the prorogation of parliament until October 1781 left him and the rest of the Patriot leadership, whose focus was the parliamentary session and whose *locus operandi* was the house of commons, unsure what to do next. Lord Charlemont, Grattan's *eminence grise*, was less hesitant than most. He was quietly optimistic that the 1781–2 session would bring success because Henry Flood, who had finally broken with the Castle after an unhappy and unfruitful term as vice-treasurer, was itching to take up the cause of legislative independence. Charlemont was confident that if the Volunteers could be induced to instruct 'their representatives' to support motions in favour of legislative independence, then the combined impact of Grattan's and Flood's oratory in the house of commons would overcome anything the Castle could put up against them.[18] The part of the plan involving the Volunteers was initiated with some success in the summer of 1781 following the recall of Buckinghamshire. However, it was soon overtaken by events as it emerged that the new lord lieutenant, the Earl of Carlisle, and his chief secretary, William Eden, were a more formidable combination than their predecessors and that the Patriots would not have it all their own way in the house of commons.

When M.P.s reassembled in Dublin in October 1781 for the new session, it quickly became apparent that the wily Eden had capitalised to such an extent on the unease within the Anglo-Irish elite with the demand for legislative independence that the administration could face parliament with confidence. With a support base of between 140 and 160 members, the Castle was able to reject motions by Grattan and Flood seeking to limit the duration of the mutiny bill and to deal comfortably with the other issues—the Portuguese trade, the tenure of judges, *habeas corpus* and the supply and money bills—raised by the opposition. They were greatly assisted in this task by defections from the Patriot benches. The succession of Barry Barry to his brother's title and the decisions of Denis Daly and Gervaise Bushe to forgo opposition for the lucre of government office had a seriously debilitating impact. To make matters worse, the remaining Patriots displayed little of the unity of purpose that had made them such a force in 1779–80. The disequilibrium caused by the loss of Barry, Daly and Bushe partly accounts for this; but the decision of Barry Yelverton to pursue his objective of amending Poynings' Law in tandem with the administration and the re-emergence of the independent-minded and not very well-liked figure of Henry Flood on the opposition benches ensured that there was no possibility of reconstructing the united front that had operated with such success in 1779.

Grattan's priorities for the session, he explained to the First Newry Regiment of Volunteers in December 1781, were the

enactment of an annual mutiny bill and the achievement of
constitutional equality with Britain.[19] At the time he made this
pronouncement the likelihood of the Patriots' securing any redef-
inition of the Anglo-Irish constitutional nexus in the short term
seemed remote. Flood and Grattan appear to have agreed a loose
working arrangement. But the rejection by the house of commons
on 11 December of Flood's motion for the establishment of a
'committee to examine precedents and records to explain the
Law of Poynings' and the acceptance some weeks later of the
heads of a bill drafted by Yelverton as the basis for a solution to
this contentious issue indicate just how isolated they had become.

The defection of Yelverton to the administration was a devel-
opment of enormous importance, for it highlighted the growing
rift within the Patriot interest as to the meaning of legislative
independence. Yelverton's preference was to amend Poynings'
Law in order to deny the Irish Privy Council the right to alter Irish
bills and to provide that only such legislation as was returned
from England with the Great Seal attached became law. Flood, by
contrast, favoured the more controversial course of a declaratory
act which conceded that the intervention of the British and Irish
Privy Councils in the Irish legislative process was founded on a
misinterpretation of the law. Grattan said little on this matter at
this time, but if his later actions are an accurate guide to his
thinking at this time, there is reason to believe that he regarded
Yelverton's proposal as entirely satisfactory. This certainly seemed
the more likely outcome as 1781 drew to a close; it also seemed
likely that neither Grattan nor Flood would be in a position to
influence events and that no resolution to the Patriots' dissatisfaction with the Declaratory Act and the Mutiny Act would be forthcoming. However, as in 1779, the Volunteers were not prepared
to stand idly by and their intervention proved decisive once more.
The decision of the Ulster corps to convene a delegate meeting in
Dungannon on 15 February 1782 to determine how best 'to root
out corruption and court influence from the legislative body'
animated what up till then had been a distinctly disappointing
session for the Patriot interest in the house of commons.[20]

Given their inability to influence the course of events in parliament, it was entirely logical that Grattan, Charlemont and Flood
should seek to steer proceedings at Dungannon assembly in a

direction that boosted their prospects of achieving a break-
through on constitutional issues. With this object in view, they
drafted two propositions for approval by the delegates. The first,
which was the handiwork of Grattan and reflected his preoccupa-
tion with the Mutiny Act and (by extension) with the Declaratory
Act, denied the right of anybody but the king, lords and commons
of Ireland to make laws for Ireland. The second, which was urged
by Flood, asserted that the interference of 'the Privy Council of
both kingdoms under, or under colour or pretence of the Law of
Poynings are unconstitutional and a grievance'. In addition, but
unknown to Charlemont and Flood, who were less disposed to
favour Catholic aspirations, Grattan also transmitted a third
resolution urging the further 'relaxation of the penal laws against
our Roman Catholic fellow subjects'.[21] This was a very significant
démarche. In 1778 Grattan had objected to the suggestion that
Catholics should be allowed to purchase land on fee-simple terms
on the grounds that it would, in the course of time, ensure that all
'the lands of the country must be in the possession of the Roman
Catholics'.[22] Four years later he had shed these apprehensions.
He was eager now to apply a definition of the concept of an 'Irish
nation' that was more religiously and demographically inclusive
than that traditionally applied by Irish Protestants, who had long
conceived of it in terms of themselves alone. Grattan's object, in
short, in 1782 was to effect more than just a revolution in Anglo-
Irish constitutional relations; he aspired also to hasten the devel-
opment of a politically less sectarian society.

The ratification of Grattan's and Flood's resolutions by the
assembly of delegates at Dungannon did not, on its own,
reanimate the faltering Patriot campaign for legislative independence in the house of commons. Indeed, motions by Grattan and
Flood in support of this claim were soundly defeated in late
February. However, the Dungannon resolutions provided
Volunteer corps throughout the country with a coherent
programme around which they could rally, so that when the
ministry of Lord North fell on 20 March the new Whig government, which had supported the Irish Patriots while in opposition,
was ill-circumstanced to withstand the growing public clamour for
legislative independence.

For Grattan and Charlemont, the succession of the Whigs to
power brought the expectation of an immediate concession of

constitutional freedom. They were able to communicate openly with Lord Rockingham and Charles James Fox—the principals in the new government. Thus when the two men, and their appointee to the lord lieutenancy of Ireland—the Duke of Portland—appealed to this openness to win time to develop an Irish policy, Grattan and Charlemont (Flood, who was disliked by the Whigs, had returned to his country seat) rejected all invitations to delay or to temper their demands. Grattan had promised M.P.s during an adjournment debate on 14 March that when parliament reconvened on 16 April he would move for an Irish declaration of rights which would call explicitly for the 'relinquishment . . . by the British parliament' of its claims to and legislative jurisdiction in Ireland, for an annual mutiny bill, and for the modification of Poynings' Law in a manner that abolished the right of the Irish Privy Council to alter or to respite Irish bills, and he was determined to keep that promise. He did. When M.P.s assembled on 16 April, he overcame illness to make one of the finest speeches of his career in favour of precisely such a programme. His sentiments were greeted rapturously, and approved unanimously. The government endeavoured to slow matters down, but Grattan refused to enter into any discussion of what he termed Ireland 'rights'. As a result, the government was forced to back down, and before the end of May the constitutional changes that gave the Irish parliament legislative independence were approved.[23]

Though Grattan declined further invitations from the government to negotiate a 'final adjustment' of Anglo-Irish relations in 1782, he had no wish to weaken the Anglo-Irish connection. His goal was the traditional Protestant nationalist one of constitutional equality for the kingdom of Ireland with Britain under the crown, not the dissolution of the British connection, as he made unambiguously clear on 16 April:

> The Crown of Ireland is an imperial crown inseparably annexed to the crown of Great Britain . . . and . . . the people of this kingdom have never expressed a desire to share the freedom of England without declaring a determination to share her fate likewise with the British nation.[24]

Most Irish Protestants shared these sentiments. Grattan was the hero of the hour; and the decision of the house of commons to vote him £50,000 in recognition of his efforts, to be used for the purchase of an estate and the construction of a 'suitable mansion', highlights the sense of euphoria that characterised the national mood in the early summer of 1782.

The readiness of M.P.s to vote Grattan such a substantial sum relieved him of financial worry for the rest of his life and seemed to herald even greater achievements in the future. However, he was not to enjoy his moment of triumph for long, as there was a small but influential number of dissentients, led by the egregious Henry Flood, who contended that the model of legislative independence proposed and accepted by Grattan was flawed and incomplete because Britain had not 'unequivocally and expressly' renounced its claim to legislate for Ireland and had retained the power to legislate on 'external' matters.[25] There was some merit in Flood's argument, but Grattan was anxious not to pursue the point. He believed the question of legislative independence was resolved, and he was eager to move forward to a less confrontational era in Anglo-Irish relations.

Personally as well as politically, Flood's decision to query what he termed 'simple repeal' could not have come at a worst time for Grattan. He was still not in full health, and he was no match for Flood in the intellectual cut-and-thrust that characterised the debate on the issue. Grattan and Charlemont endeavoured to counter slippage in support for their position by rallying the Volunteers to their cause, but the movement was all the other way. Perhaps realising the inevitable, Grattan appears simply to have abandoned the struggle. His decision towards the end of July to leave the country to take the waters at Spa left Flood free to capitalise on growing Irish fears, and he forced the British government to yield to his pressure and to 'recognise' the legislative independence of the Irish parliament in the spring of 1783.

Grattan's inability to convince the Volunteers and the public at large of the correctness of this stance on 'simple repeal' prompted a dramatic decline in his popularity before the end of 1782. More importantly, it deprived him of an obvious role in Irish politics. He had been displaced in the affections of the public by Flood; and having declined an offer of office from the Duke of Portland, he now faced the new parliamentary environment, which he had done so much to bring about, in an

unexpectedly powerless position. However, his personal circumstances were much improved. The £50,000 he was awarded by the
Irish parliament enabled him to purchase a substantial estate in
Queen's County and a residence in County Wicklow in the vale of
Tinnehinch. It also allowed him to marry; Henrietta Fitzgerald
provided him with the stable and rewarding family environment
he desired for the remainder of his life.

3

GRATTAN AND 'GRATTAN'S PARLIAMENT', 1783–1800

I

The years immediately following the winning of legislative independence proved extremely difficult politically for Henry Grattan. Emotionally and politically, he felt well-inclined to the Whigs for what they had done for Ireland in 1782, so that when they joined in a coalition government with Lord North in 1783 he was disposed to support them. He rejected the suggestion that he should serve as 'minister . . . without any employment',[26] but he did attend a number of 'cabinet' meetings in the run-up to the opening of the 1783–4 parliamentary session, though this strained his delicate relationship with Lord Charlemont, who was not prepared to compromise his political independence. Grattan, for his part, had utterly unrealistic views of how the administration should operate. He imagined it could rely on 'independent gentlemen' like himself.[27] But M.P.s of this outlook were unreliable precisely because they were 'independent'. However, nobody else had a clearer idea, and it was no surprise that the administration stumbled from crisis to crisis in the commons in the autumn and early winter of 1783 or that Grattan proved a sore disappointment to the lord lieutenant, Lord Northington, who had hoped that he would take an active part in presenting and defending government business. Grattan was in a 'no win' situation at this time. When he supported the administration, as he did on the question of maintaining an army establishment of 15,000, he was roundly criticised by the popular press for betraying his liberal principles; his opposition to protective duties, for instance, led to a mob attack on his Dublin home. *Per contra*, when he took a popular position, as he did on the questions of the duty on imported sugars and parliamentary reform, he was assailed by the administration for opposing government policy.

The issue of parliamentary reform provides a fine illustration of Grattan's predicament. In principle, he was well disposed to the reform of the Irish representative system which, he conceded, was elitist and unfair, but he believed it was not an appropriate issue for the Volunteers to agitate. For this reason, he kept the reform movement at a distance in the summer and autumn of 1783. However, when the reform bill drafted by the Grand National Convention of Volunteer delegates was presented to the house of commons in November, he antagonised not only the proponents of the measure by assailing the Volunteers for attempting to exert illegal pressure on parliament, but also its more numerous opponents by voting to receive the measure.

Grattan demonstrated a similar lack of concern for orthodox political proprieties in his relations with Henry Flood. Unable to forgive his 'hated rival' for upstaging him in 1782,[28] Grattan bore Flood a deep and festering malice which he sought to purge with a vitriolic personal attack in the house of commons on 29 October. The intervention of the law authorities ensured that no blood was spilled when Flood subsequently challenged him to a duel, but most impartial observers were in no doubt that Grattan was the aggressor.

Despite the difficulties he experienced in adjusting to the new political environment, Grattan's willingness to extend what he described, somewhat imprecisely, as 'general and sincere support' to Dublin Castle survived Lord Northington's resignation in January 1784.[29] It was not unmotivated. His priority in the spring of 1784 was the reform of the revenue administration, and for this he needed the support of the Castle phalanx in parliament. He had taken up this issue in 1783, and it was his first attempt at constructive government, but he proved unequal to the challenge because of his inability to grasp the intricacies of fiscal administration. Grattan's other reason for maintaining a working relationship with Dublin Castle was his increased alienation from his quondam allies, the Volunteers and political radicals, who continued to agitate the cause of parliamentary reform. Officially he observed an independent stance on the issue, but his support in January 1785 for a Castle initiative to abolish the Volunteers, whom he now termed the 'armed beggary',[30] indicates just how far he had distanced himself from the political agenda of the middle-class activists who directed the reform movement.

Grattan's relationship with Dublin Castle was not built on solid foundations, however, and it was not destined to last. When

Prime Minister Pitt sought in 1785 to neutralise the implications of legislative independence by binding Britain and Ireland in a commercial union, the limits of Grattan's relationship with Dublin Castle were quickly revealed. At the outset his support was secured by the Castle's willingness to amend the scheme in order to meet his objections to the proposition that the Irish parliament should make a financial contribution to imperial expenditure: it was agreed that the contribution should be contingent on the Irish budget balancing. However, when Pitt subsequently incorporated a provision obliging Ireland to maintain a uniform code of commercial regulation with Britain, Grattan broke with the administration. He deemed the proposal 'subversive of the true trade and free constitution of Ireland' and threw himself fully into the opposition camp.[31] He was even persuaded by John Forbes to effect a reconciliation with Lord Charlemont and to co-operate in parliament with Henry Flood to maximise the effectiveness of the opposition in parliament. Together they were able to convince a large enough number of M.P.s to support them that Pitt was obliged to abandon the centrepiece of his Irish policy in the 1780s.

Grattan's participation in the opposition to Pitt's plan for a commercial union had a quite dramatic impact on his political career. For nearly three years he had devoted more time to working with rather than against Dublin Castle. His actions in 1785 propelled him, at a stroke, back into the centre of opposition politics. Superficially, little had changed. He affirmed his determination to maintain an independent stance, for example by refusing to have anything to do with the attempts that were made in 1785 to establish an Irish Whig party. However, from this time onwards his allegiances lay firmly in the camp of the political opposition, and it was not long before he was once again both *persona non grata* with Dublin Castle and the key figure in the opposition to its policies in the house of commons.

II

Grattan's return to the opposition benches did not have a significant impact on the course of Irish politics in the short term. The opposition was too weak 'both in members and in concert' to cause the administration any difficulties in the house of commons

in 1786, 1787 or 1788.[32] His closest collaborator during these
years was John Forbes, the gifted but unassuming M.P. for
Drogheda. Forbes's priority was the reduction of the pension list,
but neither he nor Grattan were able to register any progress on
this issue. Grattan, likewise, was disappointed in his attempt in
1787 to make political capital out of the Navigation Act because
he 'incautiously committed himself on the subject before he
perfectly comprehended it'.[33] His main political concern during
these years was tithe reform. He took up this issue in response to
the outbreak of Rightboy violence in Munster, but successive
proposals for tithe commutation and exemptions for 'barren
lands' between 1787 and 1789 excited intense opposition from
the clergy of the Church of Ireland and the proponents of the
politics of 'Protestant ascendancy', who were determined to
preserve the 'Protestant constitution' unaltered in 'church and in
state'. As a result, Grattan's 'wonderfully able and animated'
efforts on this issue in the house of commons came to naught.[34]

Just as matters appeared at their most unpromising, the parliamentary opposition were offered a vista on power when the
incapacition of George III by mental illness in the winter of
1788–9 sparked of a constitutional crisis over the powers to be
granted the Prince of Wales should a regency prove necessary.
Grattan was in Bath with his wife when George III's breakdown
was made public. Realising the possibilities, he promptly set out
for London to consult with the Prince of Wales and his friends in
the Whig party on the course of action he should take. The Whigs
were anxious to ensure that the regent's powers should be as
broadly defined as possible because they perceived that it was
their most immediate route to office. And Grattan determined to
do what he could to support them in this cause, having received
assurances that he would be given an opportunity to reform the
basis of administration in Ireland if the Whigs obtained the reins
of power.

Excited by the prospect of making legislative independence a
working reality, Grattan capitalised on the unpopularity of the
lord lieutenant (the Marquis of Buckingham) and mass defections from the Castle ranks on his return to Dublin to pilot a
series of resolutions through the house of commons in early 1789
which offered the regency of Ireland to the Prince of Wales on

the most generous of terms. Grattan urged this course, in the teeth of strong criticism from the attorney general. But such was his ascendancy that he was even able to win majorities for votes censuring the lord lieutenant and confining the capacity of Dublin Castle to have recourse to patronage.

Unfortunately for Grattan's ambitions, George III recovered before a regency could be instituted, and the political initiative swung back to Dublin Castle. This was the worst possible outcome for many of those who had forsaken the administration on the issue, but Grattan emerged from the 'crisis' with his reputation and profile much enhanced. The 'regency crisis' re-established him as the leading opposition spokesman in the house of commons, while his concert with the Whigs on the issue broke down his longstanding antipathy to party affiliation. The Irish advocates of a regency emerged from the crisis with a party label—that of Irish Whigs—and a party structure—the Whig Clubs—and a party programme (drafted by Grattan) which committed members to the maintenance of the Irish constitution as 'settled' in 1688 and 1782, the preservation of the British connection, and the eradication of political corruption.[35]

Buoyed up by events in 1788–9, Grattan and John Forbes renewed their campaign to limit the freedom of Dublin Castle to use place and pension for the purpose of maintaining a working majority in the house of commons. With an invigorated opposition capable of bringing between eighty and a hundred M.P.s into the division lobbies, Grattan spoke energetically during the 1790 session in support of curbing 'the great increase in ministerial influence and corruption'. For the first time in many years the opposition in the house of commons resembled 'a *phallanx* [sic] [rather than] a rope of sand', but they were still insufficiently numerous to register any legislative success, and, like its predecessors, the session concluded in failure.[36]

Though the 1790 session was disappointing in legislative terms, Grattan's return to represent the Dublin city constituency in the 1790 general election offered some compensation. Grattan had long aspired to represent County Dublin in the house of commons, but he was unwilling to commit the large sums necessary to satisfy this ambition. However, following his dominant performance during the regency crisis, opinion in the capital came to believe that he was an ideal city representative, and he secured the return despite a viciously personalised campaign waged against him by the Castle press.

The reanimation of public opinion manifested during the Dublin election was a by-product of the radicalising impact of the example of the French revolutionaries on the country's middle classes. This created an atmosphere more conducive to Grattan's brand of politics than the essentially reactionary atmosphere of the late 1780s. The Whig Club, to which Grattan served as secretary for a time in 1790, prospered in this environment, but the Castle's majority in the house of commons was undisturbed. As was their practice, Grattan and Forbes consulted extensively before the opening of the new session in January 1791 on the issues—place and responsibility bills and the East India Company's charter—which they intended raising in parliament, but once again their efforts were of no avail.

While a majority of M.P.s continued to act as if nothing had happened, developments with enormous implications for the future were taking place outside parliament. By mid-1791 events in France had galvanised the middle classes to press for the redress of their grievances. The first organisation to articulate its demands was the Catholic Committee, but when it approached M.P.s in December 1791 it could get no one, Grattan included, to present its petition to parliament. The re-emergence of the Catholic question confronted Grattan with an acute political problem, though he was personally well disposed to the Catholics' aspiration for relief. His preference was to keep the issue at a distance because of the hostility of some members of the Whig Clubs and many of his Dublin constituents to any dilution of what they now termed 'Protestant ascendancy'. Thus when he was called upon by the mayor, sheriff, commons and citizens of Dublin in January 1792 to oppose any further relief to Catholics, he responded with the ambiguous affirmation: 'I love the Roman Catholic—I am a friend to his liberty—but it is only in as much as his liberty is entirely consistent with your ascendancy, and an addition to the strength and freedom of the Protestant community'.[37] Though clearly an attempt to have it both ways, this delphic avowal did not satisfy Grattan's constituents. Moreover, he was not able to maintain this stance for long. The administration's decision to offer the Catholics a modest measure of relief—access to the bar, the right to intermarry with Protestants, greater freedom in educational and commercial life—put the issue at the top of the domestic political agenda and obliged Grattan to define his position. He did so in mid-February in a series of carefully nuanced speeches in which he came out firmly in support of 'the removal of all disabilities', including the prohibition on voting, in order 'to make the Catholic a freeman and the Protestant a people'.[38]

Grattan's hesitant but explicit embrace of the cause of Catholic relief won him applause in liberal and Catholic circles. However, Catholics were extremely disappointed with the terms of the 1792 relief act, and they pressed forward through the summer and autumn with an energetic campaign to secure access to the franchise. Grattan was kept apprised of developments by Wolfe Tone, the Catholic Committee's agent, and gave generously of his advice and goodwill whenever the opportunity arose. Like the British government, he perceived concession as a means of securing Catholic loyalty in the event of a war with France, and of reducing the attraction of 'doctrines pernicious to freedom and dangerous to monarchial government' currently being propagated in France which were proving so alluring to the United Irishmen and other radicals.[39] Consequently he warmly welcomed the government's announcement of its decision to concede them the vote in 1793, and he was among the most active supporters of the measure in the house of commons.

As his mounting concern with the dissemination of radicalism highlights, Grattan kept *au fait* with the activities of the United Irishmen after this organisation was founded in 1791. His politics were distinctly more moderate, as he publicly reaffirmed when he joined the Duke of Leinster's foundation, the Friends of the Constitution, in January 1793. It was at this time also that he took up the cause of parliamentary reform. Grattan had a record of supporting parliamentary reform dating back to the early 1780s, but his sudden embrace of the issue in 1793, after many years of silence, is testimony also, as Thomas Bartlett has suggested,[40] to an opportunistic element in his political makeup. Like many constitutional politicians, Grattan was caught unawares by the speed with which the middle classes took up the cause of reform in the

C

winter and spring of 1792–3. And he was particularly uneasy with
the attempt of the radical leadership to replicate the political
conditions which had brought about legislative independence in
1782. He continued to believe that reform was a task best left to
M.P.s to resolve, and this accounts for his support (albeit with
reservations) for the administration's attempt to frustrate the
reformers' efforts to reanimate the Volunteers by constituting a
new National Guard, and for his forceful condemnation of their
plan to convene a national reform convention in Dungannon,
which he characterised as a threat to 'established government'.[41]
Grattan took this position because he believed passionately that
the best way forward for the country was a middle way between
radicalism and reaction. His antipathy to the United Irishmen,
whose radical activities he blamed for the weakening of the parliamentary opposition, almost equalled his antipathy to the proponents of the politics of 'Protestant ascendancy' at this time.

During much of the 1793 parliamentary session Grattan
believed he had an ally in the British government. The prepared-
ness of the ministry to sponsor the enfranchisement of Catholics
persuaded him that the crown wished to pursue a middle way,
and this was sufficient to induce him to support the Castle at
important points during the 1793 session. It did bring about
tangible results. As well as the concession of the franchise to
Catholics, several long-term policy aspirations of Grattan
himself—including a bill to limit the pension list, a place and
responsibility bill, and a barren lands bill—reached the statute
book. However, Grattan had little influence in the corridors of
power, and he was powerless to inhibit Dublin Castle's recourse to
repression. Parallel with the reformist measures of which he
approved, the administration pressed forward with a series of
bills—a militia act, a convention act, and an arms and gunpowder
act—which ensured that it was the conservativism espoused by
Dublin Castle rather than the moderate reformism espoused by
Henry Grattan which emerged from the 1793 parliamentary
session in the strongest position. The impact of this legislation,
combined with the rejection of a reform bill favoured by Grattan,
dealt a crushing blow to the hopes of moderate reformism, while
the initiation of a campaign of sustained repression aimed at
undermining the United Irishmen indicated clearly that coercion
rather than reform was the administration's preferred response.

The events of the 1793 session persuaded many radicals that Grattan and the parliamentary opposition had abandoned the people and thrown in their lot with the government. The enthusiasm with which Grattan supported the war against France and contended that Ireland's interests in the war were the same as those of Britain strengthened this conviction. The Castle, for its part, was delighted with Grattan's stance on the war because of the confusion it sowed among the rapidly contracting ranks of the opposition. Grattan did vigorously support William Ponsonby's 1794 plan for the reform of parliament, but Ponsonby's bill was lost by nearly one hundred votes. This accurately measured the weakened state of the parliamentary opposition at that moment, and seemed to indicate that the future for the brand of reformist politics Grattan espoused was distinctly unpropitious.

III

It was at this low moment in Grattan's fortunes that the most tantalising opportunity of his political career to shape the destiny of 'Grattan's parliament' came his way. By the late summer of 1794 negotiations between the Portland Whigs and William Pitt with a view to forming a coalition government neared completion. One of the conditions of the Whigs for entering office was the appointment of their nominee, Earl Fitzwilliam, to the Irish lord lieutenancy. Since Fitzwilliam's views on the administration of Ireland bore close resemblance to his own, the prospect of his appointment excited hope in Grattan that the conservative interest that had dominated the corridors of power in Ireland since 1783 would be swept away and a new, more moderate administration which would steer a middle course between conservatives and republicans instituted in its place.

Grattan first became aware of the imminence of Fitzwilliam's appointment in August. Fitzwilliam wrote to him to inform him that his goal in Ireland would be 'to purify, as far as circumstances and prudence will admit, the principles of government, in the hopes of thereby restoring to it that tone and spirit which so happily prevailed formerly' and that he looked 'to you and your friends, the Ponsonbys . . . for assistance in bringing it to bear'. Realising the possibilities, Grattan welcomed Fitzwilliam's communication as 'our redemption' and hurriedly travelled to London to advise the Whig peer on Irish affairs as Pitt and he endeavoured to reconcile their different ideas for the government of Ireland.[42]

Grattan was not directly party to these discussions, but his high standing with Edmund Burke and Fitzwilliam meant that he was involved at a high level from the outset, and that he played an important part in surmounting the Irish obstacles in the way of concluding the coalition negotiations. He was even consulted by Pitt following a difficult meeting between the prospective coalition partners on 15 October at which Pitt's desire to preserve continuity in personnel as well as policies in Ireland and Fitzwilliam's wish to engage in wholesale change was the main subject of disagreement. During their meeting Grattan made it clear to the prime minister that he believed a further liberal extension of Catholic civil rights was essential. Pitt was unhappy with this suggestion. He believed the moment was inopportune (because of the ongoing war with France) to embark on any form of radical change in Ireland, and his wishes prevailed on the first major difference—the future of Lord Chancellor Fitzgibbon—to be resolved. Grattan was as eager as Fitzwilliam and Burke to see the back of Fitzgibbon, but when it was clear by early November that Pitt was unmovable on this, he accepted the inevitable and gave way; Fitzgibbon retained his position.

As the negotiations between Fitzwilliam and Pitt wound their protracted course, Grattan's involvement and influence increased. He exercised particularly strong influence over Fitzwilliam, who credited him at one point with having convinced him that he ought to go to Ireland. No less significantly, he acted with Edmund Burke as an intermediary on his behalf in the negotiations with Pitt's lord chancellor, Lord Loughborough, which resulted in Fitzwilliam conceding that he would not pursue 'new systems' of government in Ireland 'but in concert with Mr Pitt', or replace existing office-holders other than in a 'temperate mode'.[43] While this was going on, Grattan also sought to negotiate his own 'terms' for agreeing to support Fitzwilliam in office. In tandem with George Ponsonby, he presented the cabinet in mid-November with a list of ten demands which encompassed requests for the liberalisation of Anglo-Irish trade, a reduction in the number of offices available to Dublin Castle, a range of appointments to specific positions, and agreement in principle to 'repeal all disqualifications against the Catholics', but these were rather brusquely rejected. Ministers knew that they did not have to make a deal with Grattan to secure his support. He was advised that the question of Catholic relief 'should not be brought forward by government', but it was not ruled out.[44] However, it was made clear to him as well as to Fitzwilliam that there should be prior consultation with ministers before the subject was agitated. With this course of proceedings ostensibly determined, the way was clear for Fitzwilliam to receive his seals of office.

Full of eagerness to get on with the task of administering Ireland according to his own designs, Grattan returned to Dublin in mid-December. Somewhat surprisingly, given the tenor of the discussions he had in England on the subject, he lost no time in briefing Dublin Catholics and encouraging them to reactivate their campaign for relief. At first sight, this may appear strange, since Grattan was expected to take the lead for the Castle in the house of commons in the upcoming session, but it becomes more comprehensible when one appreciates that Grattan did not see his role as that of a Castle loyalist whose duty was to follow British government instructions. His personal political objective was to secure the implementation of as much as possible of the liberal programme of reforms he and Ponsonby had presented to the cabinet, and it suited his purposes that Fitzwilliam should be met on his arrival in Ireland by a tide of calls for Catholic emancipation. Fitzwilliam, for his part, broadly shared Grattan's aspirations, so that when he was greeted on his arrival by a cacophonous chorus of demands for reform, he promptly set about dismissing conservative office-holders and replacing them with Irish Whigs. His actions shocked the Protestant establishment. Their unease was increased beyond measure by the lord lieutenant's speech on the opening of parliament which indicated that further Catholic relief was on the cards, and by the presentation, a few days later, by Henry Grattan of a petition from the Roman Catholics of Dublin seeking 'total emancipation'.[45]

Though he declined, once again, to accept government office, Grattan was in an unprecedentedly powerful position in the Fitzwilliam administration. From the opening debate in which he moved the address in answer to the lord lieutenant's speech, it was apparent that he was the administration's leading spokesman in the house of commons. He also exercised enormous influence on its legislative programme. During the early weeks of the session he played a leading part in the debates on the motions advanced by the administration on the defence of the country and the regulation of the Dublin police. These were two issues close to his heart; so too were the proposals to address the questions of Catholic education (by establishing a Catholic seminary at Maynooth) and parliamentary reform; but the subject he was most anxious about and which excited most anticipation was that of Catholic relief, because of the widespread expectation that the forthcoming legislative session would concede Catholics the right to sit in parliament.

Behind the scenes Fitzwilliam tried desperately to obtain cabinet sanction for Catholic emancipation, but it was not forthcoming. As he had endeavoured repeatedly to make clear to the lord lieutenant before his departure to Ireland, Pitt did not believe the time was right to alter the fundamentals of government policy on Ireland, so that when he was made aware that Grattan and Fitzwilliam had it in mind to press ahead with Catholic emancipation regardless, he determined to recall the headstrong lord lieutenant before he could do any more damage. However, while this decision was being arrived at, Grattan moved on 12 February 1795 for leave to bring in a bill to relieve 'persons professing the Roman Catholic religion' on the grounds that if emancipation was not conceded, the Catholics would have no reason to remain loyal to the crown and 'the first descent of ten thousand Frenchmen separates the two countries forever'.[46]

Inevitably, news of Fitzwilliam's recall appalled Grattan and his Irish Whig colleagues, who saw their hopes for a more inclusive government in Ireland cruelly dashed. Grattan was permanently embittered by the event, and his infamous answer to an address from the Catholics of Dublin, in which he justified Fitzwilliam's actions as in the best interests of the empire, and accused 'your old task-masters', now restored to power, of 'tyranny . . . rapacity, and malice', so bristled with anger that Fitzgibbon condemned it as a 'most audacious and treasonable invitation to rebellion'.[47] Grattan was now, to the extent that he had never been before, an heroic figure in the eyes of Irish

Catholics as well as reformist Protestants. He was equally a figure of 'alarm' for the large and growing number of Irish Protestants who perceived that his policies would admit their deepest enemies—the Catholics—to power and hasten the separation of Britain and Ireland.

Fitzwilliam's successor, Earl Camden, was as safe an appointee as Pitt could choose. He presided over the restoration to office of the loyal Protestants his predecessor had dismissed and the abandonment of Grattan's 'dangerous and impolitic' Catholic relief bill.[48] This apart, the 1795 session was not without legislative achievement for Grattan and his Whig colleagues. At least three important pieces of legislation to which Grattan made a significant contribution—a responsibility bill, a Catholic education bill, and a Dublin police bill—were ratified. However, what in any other year would have been perceived as a substantial achievement appeared thin and disappointing in the autumn of 1795. Grattan had invested his hopes as well as his energies in the Fitzwilliam administration. It represented his only real opportunity to give effect to his vision of administering the kingdom in a manner that acknowledged the justice of Catholic claims to full civil rights, while affirming, at the same time, the Anglo-Irish connection and preserving the essentially Protestant nature of the constitution.

Certainly the reaction of political radicals to Grattan's failure to deliver on the promises he had made in January and February 1795 was scathing. William Drennan concluded he had 'very *sillily* squandered his dignity of character and consequence'.[49] Middle-class Catholics on the whole were more forgiving, but throughout the country thousands of disillusioned activists who saw their hopes of effecting reform through constitutional means dashed threw in the towel and embraced revolutionary politics. Grattan's failure in 1795 left only one route to achieve the political changes they so desired, and that route, as Grattan had apprehended, led to France and to violence.

IV

The embrace by radicals of the principles of revolution, and the attendant explosion in lawlessness in the countryside, had the effect of reinforcing the conviction of the conservatives, who once again dominated the corridors of power, of the necessity of

further and firmer security measures. Grattan spent the latter part
of 1795 attempting to persuade Catholics to 'agitate their
grievances once more',[50] but neither the Catholic leadership nor
the parliamentary opposition had the stomach for another
campaign so soon. They were equally disinclined towards
Grattan's attempt in September to forge a grand alliance of
Whigs, Dissenters and Catholics in favour of reform. As a result,
when parliament reconvened in January 1796, Grattan sat on
virtually empty opposition benches and was powerless to resist the
administration's plan to offer an exclusively security-based
response to the mounting problems of sedition and disorder.
Every effort by the opposition to draw attention to the fact that
the civil unrest had an economic dimension and that it should
not be addressed in stark law-and-order terms was rejected. Both
Castle officials and a solid majority of M.P.s were convinced that
repression was the proper response, with the result that the
administration was able to press ahead unimpeded with its plans
for an insurrection act which gave it sweeping new powers to
combat revolutionary activity. Grattan endeavoured to convince
M.P.s that they ought to apply the same coercive measures against
Protestant Orangemen as they deemed appropriate for Catholic
Defenders, but a majority was disinclined. Not surprisingly,
Grattan's spirits began to droop, and by the conclusion of the
parliamentary session in April he was quite depressed by the state
of the country. He explained to Earl Fitzwilliam:

> On the whole, I do not remember a time less promising to
> this country. There are now two constitutions in Ireland, one
> for the rich and another for the poor . . . The war is begun in
> Ireland between property and poverty—it is commenced by
> the former on the privileges of the latter. Should a discontent
> take place, it would be retaliated by the numbers of the latter
> on the property and on the persons of the former. The
> majorities of our house have gotten the spirit of planters not
> of country gentlemen. They hate the Papist and they hate the
> people.[51]

And matters were to get worse. The 'complete command' the
administration enjoyed in the house of commons ensured that
when parliament was reconvened in the autumn of 1796 to
implement further repressive measures, Grattan's reservations fell
on deaf ears. He was now a marginalised figure in the house of

commons, as was highlighted by the crushing 149 to 12 and 143 to 19 defeats on his motions of 17 October for Catholic emancipation.

The main consequence for Grattan of the repeated failure of the house of commons to respond positively to his calls for reform was his gradual disenchantment with parliamentary politics. The failure of the Irish parliament to address what he believed were the real problems of the country and the mounting alienation of the population at large troubled him deeply. It did not, as his opponents were wont to allege, persuade him of the futility of parliamentary government. Grattan never lost faith in parliamentary government as such. But he did despair of the Irish parliament because of its continued refusal to accept 'the claim of right—the Catholic claims', which he now attributed to the failure of the 1782 constitutional settlement to provide for 'the strengthening Ireland in her own parliament by a free admission of the people'.[52] Grattan's disgruntlement climaxed during the 1797 parliamentary session following the rejection of a series of motions urged by him in favour of an absentee tax and parliamentary reform and critical of the conduct of the war with France and General Lake's ruthless disarming of Ulster. Thoroughly convinced that there was no further point in participating in parliamentary debate, he announced that he would no longer 'attend' the house of commons and he withdrew.

Grattan's secession from parliament and his subsequent decision not to stand for re-election in 1797 in protest at government actions represented the ultimate acknowledgment by the middle ground of its failure to steer a viable course between the republican separatism of the United Irishmen and the intransigent conservatism of ascendancy Protestantism. Having cut his ties with the conservative-dominated house of commons, it was logical that Grattan should gravitate towards radicalism. Indeed, Samuel Neilson attempted to recruit him into the United Irish organisation in the autumn of 1797, but Grattan was not tempted. He firmly believed that the United Irishmen's programme did not offer any solutions to the country's problems. Despite this, he was prepared to socialise with United men, and to co-operate with them on occasions. He worked, for example, with the Sampson brothers gathering material for Lord Moira to use in his attack on Pitt's Irish policy at Westminster in the spring of 1798. He also travelled to England in April of the same year to testify on behalf of his former parliamentary colleague Arthur O'Connor, who was charged with treason.

Such actions appalled conservative Protestant opinion, which accused Grattan and his allies 'of sacrificing their country to their personal resentments', and loyalist anger boiled over when the country was plunged into rebellion in May 1798.[53] Luckily for Grattan, he was in England when the rebellion broke out, otherwise he almost certainly would have been the victim of reprisal attacks. As it was, his house at Tinnehinch was searched, and a number of his servants intimidated and assaulted. In his absence, Grattan was the target of a constant stream of literary vituperation from conservative Protestants, the most irrational of which by Dr Patrick Duigenan prompted him to issue a challenge. No duel took place, but given the disposition of some conservatives to believe he was as much a 'rebel' as the Wexford insurgents and to attribute the rebellion to his actions, he wisely chose to remain in England during most of 1798. For a time, indeed, it appeared that he would be charged with complicity in the rebellion on the evidence of an informer who submitted that he had taken the United Irish oath. There was no basis to the allegation, but it did not save Grattan's reputation. He was dismissed from the Irish Privy Council by George III and expelled from the Dublin Guild of Merchants. Grattan attempted to defend his honour against the calumny that was being heaped upon it, but his opponents were so blinded by prejudice that his interventions were counterproductive.

Once the rebellion was over, attention in parliament quickly passed to Prime Minister Pitt's decision to press for the legislative union of the two kingdoms in order to preserve British authority in Ireland. Grattan, inevitably, was hostile to the idea, but because he did not have a commons seat there was little he could do to counter it. He returned to Dublin from England in January 1799 for the new parliamentary session, and he was delighted when the house of commons narrowly rejected the measure. However, this did not deflect the prime minister. Pitt instructed Cornwallis, the lord lieutenant, to secure a majority for the proposal in the 1800 session, and because of an indisposition which obliged him to spend most of the year recuperating in England, Grattan once again was not in a position to participate in the opposition campaign. He returned to Ireland late in 1799 and purchased a commons seat for the borough of Wicklow. He was still in poor health, but despite medical advice to avoid exertion, he took his seat and made an eloquent and aggressive two-hour speech on 15 January in which he declaimed at length on the undesirability of the proposed union and the misleading nature of attendant government promises. It was to no avail; the Castle had sufficiently strengthened its support base since 1799 to be in a position to defeat the opposition on this and on all subsequent occasions during the session by a comfortable margin. Grattan was invariably prominent in the ongoing opposition challenge to the government's efforts to push the bill through. He made a series of powerful emotional speeches throughout February and March (one of which led to a duel with the chancellor of the exchequer, Isaac Corry), but, as on so many occasions during the preceding decade, he was unable to bring a majority of M.P.s with him.

The optimism and confidence that had proved of such advantage to Patriot opinion in the early 1780s was in very short supply at the end of the 1790s. In 1782 Irish Protestants had grasped the opportunity represented by legislative independence. However, most were so disturbed by the 1798 rebellion, which ignited fears of a repetition of the 1641 massacres, that the security the Act of Union seemed to offer had enormous appeal. By choosing this option, they closed the door on the vision of constitutional equality with Britain which Grattan had defined so eloquently in 1782, just as firmly as they had rejected his vision of a more inclusive 'Irish nation' in the 1790s.

The ratification of the Act of Union brought an end to the constitutional experiment known today as 'Grattan's parliament'. In truth, Grattan exercised only marginal influence on its deliberations throughout its eighteen-year existence. He did have a number of opportunities to play a more influential role in political decision-making. But his unwillingness to accept the responsibilities of office in 1782–3, his inability to master detail, poor judgment and bad luck ensured that real power throughout the 1780s and 1790s remained in the possession of Dublin Castle and the representatives of the Protestant ascendancy whom London deemed it more appropriate to entrust with positions of responsibility.

4

CATHOLIC EMANCIPATOR, 1801–20

After the enactment of the Act of Union, Grattan retired from political life for a number of years. He devoted his life to study, to his family and to estate matters, and only kept in touch with political developments through friends and the press. He remained committed to the cause of Catholic emancipation, but the atmosphere of animosity and suspicion in the early years of the new century was unconducive to progress on this issue. The failure of William Pitt's attempt to steer a Catholic relief bill through the Westminster parliament in 1801 because of George III's opposition was a serious setback, but Grattan declined to make any public pronouncement. He was less able to conceal his unease with the seditious activities of the remnants of the United Irishmen. Grattan's antipathy to the aims of what he termed the 'separation party' had intensified as a consequence of events in the late 1790s, and he was appalled by the 'stupidity' and 'barbarity' of Robert Emmet's *émeute* of 1803.[54]

Grattan was of the opinion that only a complete change in the tone and tenor of government would restore harmony to Irish life. Specifically, he urged the 'cordial execution by the executive magistrates of the laws in favour of Catholics', the appointment of Catholics 'to a share in offices to which they are now qualified' and, most of all, Catholic emancipation.[55] Consequently, when Charles James Fox's initiative to reanimate the Catholic question in the autumn of 1804 received support from the Catholic leadership in Ireland, he was persuaded to accept a nomination from Earl Fitzwilliam for the borough of Malton in Yorkshire in April 1805 in order to support the Catholic petition at Westminster.

Grattan's decision to enter the house of commons at Westminster was not without risk. He was fifty-nine years old and committed to present a petition which everybody anticipated would be rejected. Undaunted by this, he prepared for the occasion with his usual thoroughness; and when called upon by the speaker, he made a powerful and convincing contribution in support of the Catholic petition and against the harsh invective of his long-time antagonist, Patrick Duigenan, who articulated the view of many Protestants that Catholics could not be emancipated because 'they could not be faithful subjects to a Protestant monarchy'. His speech was a *tour de force*. He exposed the inherent bigotry and intolerance of Duigenan's invective with such dexterity that even Pitt was moved.[56] It did not prevent the rejection of the petition, but that apart, the occasion was a personal triumph for Grattan.

The impact of Grattan's 'début in parliament' won him great credit with the advocates of Catholic emancipation on both sides of the Irish Sea and revitalised his political career. He was elected to represent the Dublin city constituency once more in 1806, and he was offered the chancellorship of the Irish exchequer when his English allies succeeded to power in the same year. Once again he declined the responsibilities of office. He was not suited, he now realised, to administration. He did, however, welcome his reappointment to the Privy Council, and anticipated that the accession to power of Charles James Fox and Lord Grenville would produce more benign and sympathetic government in Ireland. Fox pronounced himself well inclined, but the moment was inopportune, as Grattan and he both appreciated, to press for Catholic emancipation. Grattan used his influence with the Irish Catholics to persuade them not to embarrass the ministry by agitating a petition, for he was optimistic that progress could be made in other areas. However, it was not to be. He was taken aback when a modest measure of relief aimed at improving access for Catholics to the armed forces, which he encouraged the government to undertake, resulted in the dismissal of the ministry from office by the king, and its replacement by a government headed by the Duke of Portland, which was committed to oppose Catholic relief.

Grattan had little time for Portland, but, despite this, he justified the new ministry's decision to press ahead with insurrection and arms acts to combat disorder in Ireland as 'necessary' action. Grattan's readiness to support these measures was in accord with his conviction that the upsurge in rural disorder at this time was the work of a 'French party' and that this had to be eradicated if any progress was to be made in the resolution of the country's problems. However, it did not save him from fierce domestic criticism, where there was sheer amazement that he should support legislation which would result, one critic averred, in the destruction of 'thousands'.[57]

Grattan's failure to back Catholic petitions for emancipation in 1807, as well as his support for the government's arms and insurrection acts did his reputation little permanent harm. He was invited once again to present a Catholic petition in 1808, but there were doubts in pro-emancipation quarters as to the merit of such a course without some concession to allay the fears of the influential 'No Popery' interest in the house of commons. The most obvious gesture was to grant the crown a negative veto in the appointment of Catholic bishops, since this had been agreed in principle by the hierarchy in 1799. Grattan was briefed on this subject by George Ponsonby, and he was so convinced it represented a way forward that he made it a central feature of his speech in favour of the Catholic petition he presented to the house of commons on 25 May 1808. Unfortunately it set back rather than enhanced the cause he advocated. In the first place, it did not secure the acceptance of the petition. More seriously, it excited an enormous stir in Ireland, where Catholic opinion divided into pro- and anti-veto wings and, ominously, the bishops came out publicly against any involvement by the crown in their appointment. Grattan was informed personally of the bishops' objections when he returned to Dublin in September, and he did not like what he heard. He realised that the dispute had done the emancipation cause damage in Britain, and he concluded there was no point pressing the question in the forthcoming session.

Grattan was able to make this judgment with some authority because he was now firmly established as one of the leading members of the Whig party at Westminster. Reflecting this rise in stature, he took a more active role in parliamentary debate in the 1809 session than in preceding years. He was prominent in the Whigs' efforts to secure economic reform, and in their motions censuring the Duke of York and Lord Castlereagh for 'corrupt practices'. One of the consequences of his ascent up the Whig hierarchy was the need to spend more time in England. Grattan now derived greater pleasure from his annual sojourns to

Westminster than he had when first elected to the united parliament because of his widening circle of English friends. Grattan was highly regarded as a dinner companion, sage counsellor and political adviser by a growing circle of hostesses and opposition politicians, and they provided him with plenty of opportunities to display his wisdom and sociability during his visits to England.

Meanwhile the differences engendered by the veto issue within the broad alliance of Catholics and liberal Protestants that supported Catholic emancipation continued, as Grattan had apprehended, to damage its credibility. Those well disposed to emancipation were encouraged to renew their campaign in 1810 by reports of the deterioration in the health of George III, which raised the likelihood of a regency headed by the Prince of Wales and the appointment of a pro-Catholic administration. At the invitation of the Catholic Committee, Grattan undertook to present a petition requesting relief. But his relations with the Catholic leadership, never very close, were put under renewed strain when he stated to the house of commons that he could no longer stand over his 1808 statement that the Catholics would accept a veto on ecclesiastical nomination and, in an otherwise 'admirable' defence of Catholic rights, expressed himself in favour of 'the domestic nomination of Catholic bishops'.[58] This attempt by Grattan to identify a middle way between Catholic resistance to the veto in any form and Protestant antipathy to the principle of unrestricted papal nomination added a new dimension to the troubled veto issue, but it won few supporters in either camp.

Having failed once again to identify a *via media* acceptable to pro and anti-emancipists, Grattan returned to Tinnehinch in June 1810, delighted to escape 'the expense of England *and the vagabond life which I am obliged to live*'.[59] However, Ireland proved less restful than he had hoped, as a combination of economic difficulties and mounting disenchantment with the Act of Union gave rise to calls in Dublin for the establishment of a repeal movement. One of the most enthusiastic advocates of such a course was Henry Grattan junior. He aspired to follow in the political footsteps of his father, but Grattan senior effectively quashed his ambitions by forbidding him to attend the county meeting called to launch the campaign. Grattan senior was disinclined to have anything to do with a campaign to repeal the Act of Union he believed could not succeed. He responded tactfully to calls on him 'to be unwearied in his endeavours to have its legislature restored to this ill-fated country', but he did nothing to encourage them, and they quickly subsided.[60]

Grattan was more hopeful about Catholic emancipation, though his relations with the Catholic Committee remained testy. Rumours that the Committee's dissatisfaction with his comments on the veto in 1810 would prompt them to invite another M.P. to present their petition to the House of Commons in 1811 proved false, and Grattan amply repaid their continued trust by making a vigorous speech in support of their claims on 31 May. It was rejected by a substantial margin, but, despite this, Grattan confidently anticipated success 'when the prince comes to the throne', and this may explain his rather brusque refusal in June to present another Catholic petition objecting to a clause in the militia bill on the grounds that it was 'not presentable'.[61]

Grattan's independent-mindedness exasperated Irish Catholics at times, but they generally contained their anger and came back to him because he was their most influential voice in the house of commons. Prospects for Catholic relief certainly appeared better in 1812 than they had been for many years. Grattan was confident that it was just a matter of time before the Prince Regent invited the Whigs to take office, and his hopes were buoyed by the support his so-called 'Protestant petition' garnered in Ireland. Encouraged by this, Grattan spoke lyrically in support of the necessity of the unconditional concession of emancipation to Catholics in a debate on 'the state of Ireland' on 3 February, and he was characteristically impressive in moving for a committee to consider the laws in force against Catholics on 23 April. Both motions were lost by a considerable margin, but the fact that the pro-emancipation side secured 215 votes represented progress and won Grattan renewed praise from Irish Catholics.

Much more important for the future of Catholic emancipation was the composition of the government. To Grattan's dismay, it emerged that the Prince Regent's preference was for a government that opposed Catholic claims. This ruled out the Whigs and led to the accession to power of the conservative peer Lord Liverpool, who was quite happy to follow his sovereign's wishes on the question. In spite of this setback, Grattan resolved to press on. It was agreed by all sides that 'the Catholic question [w]as in Grattan's hands',[62] and heartened by the increase in support in recent years for emancipation in the house of commons, he was optimistic for the 1813 session. He had cause. On 25 February he moved that a parliamentary committee be established to draft a Catholic relief bill with appropriate 'securities' to safeguard the Protestant succession and the Protestant church. This provoked a marathon debate spanning four days, but in the end Grattan emerged victorious by forty votes. Emboldened by this, he pressed onward and in the teeth of fierce opposition from hardline Protestants whose anti-Catholicism was unallayable, he won successive divisions in committee before securing leave to introduce a bill on 30 April. As he had predetermined with his closest Irish advisers the previous December, the Catholic relief bill of 1813 was a relatively simple measure. Instead of taking the expected and convoluted route of identifying and repealing the many anti-Catholic laws still on the statute book, it provided that Catholics should be eligible to hold every position except the monarchy, the lord lieutenancy of Ireland and the lord chancellorship, provided they took an oath of allegiance swearing to uphold the Protestant succession, the Protestant church and Protestant property, and rejected the nomination to the Catholic episcopacy of anyone whose loyalty was not unimpeachable.

This was a disarmingly straightforward piece of legislation, but it did not protect the measure against fierce criticism. Grattan managed to overcome Sir John Coxe Hippisley's delaying motion on 11 May, but he was powerless to resist amendments by George Canning and Lord Castlereagh vesting the nomination of Catholic bishops in the crown. More significantly, when Speaker Abbot moved on 24 May 'to leave out the words giving the Roman Catholics a right to sit and vote for the two houses of parliament' and his amendment was carried by the narrow margin of four votes, Grattan realised that his spirited attempt to win emancipation had failed and he withdrew the bill.[63] To add to his troubles, the Catholic bishops of Ireland joined in the criticism of his initiative by condemning his bill a few days later as utterly incompatible with the discipline of their church.

The emasculation of the 1813 relief act, the proscription in 1814 of the Catholic Board, and the deep divisions created within

D

the Irish Catholic body politic by the veto issue and the rescript of papal nuncio Quarantotti, which was seen to support the pro-veto side on the subject of ecclesiastical nomination, effectively undermined any hopes Grattan might have entertained of renewing the campaign for Catholic emancipation in the short term. He did present a number of Catholic petitions to the house of commons in 1814, but he did not speak in support of any of them because he did not believe the moment propitious.

Relations between Grattan and the Catholic leadership were distinctly frosty throughout 1814 and 1815. They had become strained in late 1813 following Grattan's objection to what he believed was an attempt by the Catholic Board to 'dictate' to him the terms of any future Catholic relief bill he should promote. He was not entrusted with their petition in 1815 on the insistence of the anti-veto side. Moreover, prospects of an early accommodation seemed remote in the wake of his pronouncement in the house of commons in May that the 'Roman Catholics [could] not hope for relief till they . . . offered securities, which he thought not to be essential . . ., in deference to the feelings of their Protestant countrymen'.[64] Indeed, prospects for emancipation disimproved further when the Catholic leadership split into pro- and anti-veto factions. Both drafted petitions for presentation to the house of commons in 1816 (Grattan presented that of the pro-veto side), but to nobody's surprise neither made progress. There were, of course, calls, notably by Sir Henry Parnell (who had been entrusted with the Catholic petition in 1815), for the 'two parties' to form a 'coalition', but their differences ran too deep. Parnell realised full well that Grattan was the only M.P. capable of piloting a substantial Catholic relief measure through the house of commons, but it galled the anti-vetoists, led by Daniel O'Connell and Denys Scully, that they should be dependent on someone who refused to be guided by them on this question. The fact that Grattan was not personally attached to the veto did not influence their thinking, and no reconciliation was effected by the time Grattan took the floor of the house of commons in May 1817 to move once again for a committee of the whole house to consider the laws affecting Catholics. The 'security' Grattan offered on this occasion was 'domestic nomination' and advocates of Catholic relief in the house of commons were optimistic of success. However, they did not reckon on Robert Peel, the Irish chief secretary. He carried the day by demonstrating that Grattan's compromise proposal was unworkable because many of the Irish Catholics it was designed to relieve were hostile to it. Grattan's last realistic effort to obtain what he now termed 'his dearest wish' had failed.

In the wake of his disappointment in 1817, Grattan could see no advantage in presenting another Catholic petition in 1818. His priority was his re-election for the city of Dublin, and he successfully defended his seat, though he was injured in an election riot caused by an O'Connellite mob. Shortly afterwards he and Sir Henry Parnell came together once more to consider the best way to forward the Catholic question at Westminster in 1819. There were signs momentarily that a reconciliation might be forged between the pro- and anti-vetoist interests, but the distrust of the two sides for each other was too acute for co-operation to prove possible. It did not make any difference. Grattan's failure to bring the subject forward at a sufficiently early date in the session effectively confined it to a single day's debate, which thwarted Henry Parnell's hopes of securing access to parliament for Catholics by the amendment of the oath of supremacy.

It was, as fate was to have it, Grattan's last major speech. Though the prospects for Catholic relief in the immediate future were perceived in some quarters as good, Grattan did not take any further part. He became seriously ill in the autumn of 1819, and though he defied medical advice and travelled to London in May 1820 with the intention of making a final plea for Catholic relief, he was too weak to take his seat. He died on 4 June without fulfilling his last political wish.

Of the many episodes in Henry Grattan's long political career, his advocacy of Catholic emancipation in the Westminster parliament is perhaps the least well known. Yet he deserves considerable credit for his persistent advocacy of the question in the face of a more powerful and concerted opposition. As in the 1790s, his efforts to identify an acceptable middle way between the Catholic proponents of unconditional emancipation and Protestant advocates of the *status quo* failed, but he did succeed in giving the cause of emancipation a high profile at Westminster and helped to erode the deep-seated resistance of British Protestant opinion to Catholic civil rights. In the process he won admiration as a man of principle and dignity. It was not altogether fitting that his remains should be interred in Westminster Abbey, but given his anxiety to maintain the Anglo-Irish connection and his effective working of the Union, it was as appropriate a mausoleum as any other.

CONCLUSION

Grattan's death, like so many of the major moments in his political career, was a highly charged and emotional affair, and he managed it with great efficiency. Grattan was a master at this. Having observed Chatham and Burke closely as a young man, he was acutely aware of the power of words, and throughout his political life he was able, through a well-chosen phrase, to excite an emotional response in his audience. Whether or not Grattan actually needed the adulation his famed oratory brought him it is difficult to say. He certainly enjoyed fame; and if it would be only slightly unfair to accuse him of vanity, it is true that he liked being the centre of attention, and it was thus from the moment he entered politics.

Grattan's rise to prominence in the late 1770s was meteoric. This was due in no small part to his oratorical skills. But of equal, if not greater, importance was his ability to articulate the grievances of the Protestant middle classes, for it was their emergence as a force in Irish political life as much as the skill of opposition spokesmen and the preoccupations of the British government in America that enabled the Patriots to achieve their political objectives. Grattan, of course, had an advantage over his rivals in that respect; unlike most of them, he had no interest in government employment and, as a result, he had no personal incentive to temper his rhetoric. This worked to his advantage for several years, and enabled him to become the leading Patriot voice in the house of commons. However, in the autumn of 1782 he was outflanked by his one-time friend and political senior, Henry Flood. As Grattan admitted on his death-bed, Flood was a man of 'great talents and abilities';[65] indeed, Flood possessed a finer mind than Grattan, although he could do little but watch from the sidelines as Grattan led the forces of Protestant nationalism to the triumphs of 'free trade' in 1780 and legislative independence in the spring of 1782.

His contribution to the winning of legislative independence was Grattan's single greatest political achievement, but it

47

appeared to him that the cup of victory was snatched from his lips by Flood's questioning of the validity of 'simple repeal'. It was at this point that Grattan's political career lost direction. He toyed with working with Dublin Castle. But the failure to follow legislative independence with parliamentary reform left the 'constitution of 1782' incomplete because it did not provide for the participation of the middle classes, whose expectations had been aroused by their important contributions to the campaigns for 'free trade' and legislative independence, and meant that there was no place in the Irish administration for an independent-minded populist like Grattan. He could possibly have put his career back onto the rails by taking a more active role in the parliamentary reform movement in 1783 and 1784, but his newly discovered unease with extra-parliamentary activity and his fierce condemnations of the Volunteers cut him off from the constituency which was his natural home. In sheer frustration, he struck out at Flood. This was an unwarranted and an unwise move, and it could have led to his untimely death, since Flood was an experienced duellist. Gradually, however, Grattan worked his way back into the public's affections and to his former position as leader of the parliamentary opposition. Pitt's commercial arrangement prompted him to break his connection with Dublin Castle, while the regency crisis of 1788–9 caused him to abandon the independent position he had occupied since 1782. In effect, he became a Whig.

Throughout the early 1790s Grattan pursued a broadly traditionalist Patriot programme. In tandem with John Forbes, he urged the Irish parliament to confine the administration's capacity to use patronage and to eradicate corruption. However, this attempt to reanimate the politics of civic humanism within existing political structures was anachronistic, because the outbreak of revolution in France, by illustrating the potential of radical political reform, brought the more fundamental questions of Catholic relief and parliamentary reform back to the top of the Irish political agenda. These two issues had been agitated without success by the reform movement of the early 1780s, when Grattan had taken a very low profile on both questions because of his alienation from popular politics as a consequence of his stance on 'simple repeal'. However, in the 1790s he came to appreciate that the goal of a more inclusive Irish nation he had articulated, but not pursued, in 1782 was the only way to make legislative independence a working reality and to prevent the country from descending into ethno-religious strife. It was for these reasons that he embraced the questions of parliamentary reform and Catholic relief in 1792–3, though by doing so he alienated himself from the bulk of the Protestant community into which he was born and on whose behalf he had pursued 'free trade' and legislative independence.

Grattan's finest opportunity to achieve these aims came with the appointment of Earl Fitzwilliam to the Irish lord lieutenancy in 1794, but it came to grief owing to the impolitic urgency with which he and Fitzwilliam sought to undo the policies of their opponents and to press forward with Catholic emancipation. Thereafter Grattan became an increasingly isolated figure in Irish politics as the conservative interest which was restored to power in Dublin Castle resorted exclusively to repression to combat the growing threat of revolutionary disorder in the countryside. Isolated in his natural theatre—the house of commons—Grattan eventually gave up the struggle and seceded in 1797. He refused, at the same time, to embrace the extra-parliamentary politics of the United Irishmen, and spent a number of unhappy years in the political wilderness in the late 1790s.

Though at the outset disinclined to play any further part in political life, following his symbolic but ineffectual opposition to the ratification of the Act of Union, Grattan's political career was revived by his re-embrace of the Catholic question and his election to the Westminster parliament in 1805.

He still possessed his famed oratorical prowess, and once he had demonstrated that his commitment to the Catholic cause was genuine, he was received graciously and treated as a valued elder statesman by the Whig interest in the house of commons. However, his approach was essentially cautious and confined to the realm of high politics. As a parliamentary politician, Grattan was no longer prepared to have recourse to extra-parliamentary agitation. He had supported the extra-parliamentary tactics of the Volunteers in the late 1770s and early 1780s, but he upheld the primacy of parliament following his criticism of the Volunteer-led campaign for parliamentary reform in 1783–4. For this reason, he never considered launching a popular agitation for Catholic

emancipation which might have given the cause the impetus it so
clearly needed, and, as a result, successive efforts to advance
emancipation between 1805 and 1819 foundered on the rocks of
Protestant intransigence and Catholic refusal to compromise.
Despite repeated rebuffs, Grattan continued to press the issue. He
summarised the political ambitions of his later life on his death-
bed as 'to preserve the connexion between the two countries and
[to] grant the Catholics their just privileges'. He believed indeed
that Britain and Ireland 'must stand together united quoad
nature—distinct quoad legislation', and though the question did
not receive an enormous amount of attention during his lifetime,
his refusal to embrace the cause of repeal in 1810 indicates that
'to preserve the connexion' was at least as important to him as to
grant 'just privileges' to Catholics.[66]

Grattan's political moderacy, personal conviviality and
inherent dislike of injustice provide three of the main reasons for
his enormous popularity during most of lifetime. His ability to
articulate the aspirations of those who sought change in an era of
major political upheaval was his greatest political asset. However,
like most moderates in an era of revolution, he discovered that his
attempt to steer a middle course between the Scylla of radicalism
and the Charybdis of conservativism ended in failure. It did so
partly because he was not a sufficiently talented politician to
navigate such a course. But the main reason, quite simply, was
that his goal of forging an 'Irish nation' which was legislatively
independent but bound under the crown to Great Britain and
which embraced the aspirations of Irish Catholics as well as Irish
Protestants was unattainable because a majority of the people in
the two kingdoms did not share it.

NOTES

[1] Gerard O'Brien, 'The Grattan mystique', *Eighteenth-Century Ireland*, i (1986), pp 190–94.

[2] Henry Grattan jr, *Memoirs of the life and times of the Rt Hon. Henry Grattan* (5 vols, London, 1839–46), i, pp vii–viii.

[3] Indenture between James Grattan and Thomas Marlay, 4 May 1740 (Public Record Office of Northern Ireland (hereafter PRONI), Fitzwilliam (Langdale) papers, Mic 71).

[4] James Grattan, *The recorder's second letter to the gentry, clergy, freemen and freeholders of the city of Dublin* (Dublin, 1758), p. 6.

[5] *Miscellaneous works of the Rt Hon. Henry Grattan* (London, 1822), p. 3.

[6] *Life of Grattan*, i, 256.

[7] National Library of Ireland (hereafter NLI), Grattan Papers, MS 3886, f. 31.

[8] Almon's *Narrative of proceedings . . . in the parliament of Ireland*, p. 36.

[9] Dublin City Library, Harcourt Papers, Gilbert MS 93, ff 375–6.

[10] A. R. Black (ed.), *An edition of the Cavendish Irish parliamentary diary, 1776–78* (3 vols, Delavan, 1984), i, 49.

[11] Thomas Prior, *The life of Edmund Malone* (London, 1860), pp 63–4.

[12] *Life of Grattan*, i, 387.

[13] *Some authentic minutes of the proceedings of a very respectable assembly on the 20th of December 1779* (Dublin, 1780), p. 39.

[14] *Grattan's miscellaneous works*, p. 143.

[15] NLI, Dobbs papers, MS 2251, f. 99.

[16] R. V. Callen, 'Cavendish's diary of the Irish parliament, October 12 1779 to September 2 1780' (Ph.D. thesis, University of Notre Dame, 1973), p. 290.

[17] Birr Castle, Rosse Papers, F/13.

[18] HMC, *Charlemont*, i, 379–80.

[19] *Grattan's miscellaneous works*, pp 169–70.

[20] R. B. McDowell, *Ireland in the age of imperialism and revolution, 1760–1801* (Oxford, 1979), pp 280–81.

[21] *Life of Grattan*, ii, 204–07.

[22] Library of Congress, Cavendish's parliamentary diary, xi, p. 284.

[23] James Kelly, *Prelude to union: Anglo-Irish politics in the 1780s* (Cork, 1992), pp 33–40.

[24] *The parliamentary register . . . . of the house of commons of Ireland* (17 vols, Dublin, 1782–1801), i, 339–40.

[25] *Life of Grattan*, ii, 345–9; William Beresford (ed.), *The correspondence of John Beresford* (2 vols, London, 1854), i, 207–11.

[26] British Library, Pelham Papers, Add. MS 33100, ff 358–9.

[27] HMC, *Fortescue*, i, 220.

[28] HMC, *Charlemont*, i, 80.

[29] *Life of Grattan*, i, 95.

[30] *Parl. reg. (Ire.)*, iv, 41.

[31] NLI, Bolton Papers, MS 16351, f. 34.

[32] PRONI, Stanhope (Pitt) papers, T3401/1/5.

[33] A. P. W. Malcomson, *John Foster: the politics of the Anglo-Irish ascendancy* (Oxford, 1978), p. 368.

[34] James Kelly, 'The genesis of Protestant ascendancy' in Gerard O'Brien (ed.), *Parliament, politics and people* (Dublin, 1989), pp 92–127; British Library, Dropmore papers, Add. MS 58969, ff 19–20.

[35] *Life of Grattan*, iii, 432–8.

[36] *Annual Register*, xxxii (1790), p. 104; Countess of Ilchester *et al.* (eds), *The life and letters of Lady Sarah Lennox* (2 vols, London, 1902), ii, 76.

[37] *Grattan's miscellaneous works*, p. 289.

[38] *Life of Grattan*, iv, 60–64.

[39] Ibid., iv, 87.

[40] Thomas Bartlett, *The fall and rise of the Irish nation* (Dublin, 1992), p. 158.

[41] D. A. Chart (ed.), *The Drennan letters* (Belfast, 1931), p. 129.

[42] *Life of Grattan*, iv, 173–4; R. B. McDowell (ed.), *The correspondence of Edmund Burke*, viii (Cambridge 1969), p. 21n.

[43] *Burke corr.*, viii, 74–6.

[44] 'The terms proposed to the cabinet by Mr Grattan, 15 November 1794' (PRONI, Fitzwilliam/Grattan Papers, T3649/8).

[45] *Burke corr.*, viii, 125.

[46] *Annual Register*, xxxvii (1795) p. 224; *Burke corr.*, vii, 150–51.

[47] *Life of Grattan*, iv, 216–24; PRONI, Sneyd Papers, T3229/1/7.

[48] Kent Archives Office, Camden Papers, U840/0127.

[49] *Drennan letters*, p. 224.

[50] Ibid., p. 229.

[51] Sheffield City Library, Fitzwilliam papers, F.30.

[52] PRONI, McPeake Papers, T3048/A/10.

[53] O'Beirne to Fitzwilliam, 6 Mar. 1798 (Sheffield City Library, Fitzwilliam papers, F.30).

[54] *Life of Grattan*, v, 223–4.

[55] Ibid., 241–2.

[56] *Annual Register*, xlvii (1805), pp 93–7.

[57] *Life of Grattan*, v, 358–62; An Irishman, *A letter to Henry Grattan on the subject of his vote on the insurrection bill . . .* (Dublin, 1807), p. 17.

[58] *Annual Register*, lii (1810), pp 133–6; Brian McDermott (ed.), *The Catholic question in Ireland and England, 1798–1822: the papers of Denys Scully* (Dublin, 1988), p. 220.

[59] *Life of Grattan*, v, 411–12.

[60] *Grattan's miscellaneous works*, pp 316–18.

[61] NLI, Grattan papers, MS 2111; *Life of Grattan*, v, 441–2.

[62] Lord Colchester (ed.), *Diary and correspondence of Charles Abbot, Lord Colchester* (3 vols, London, 1861), ii, 410–11.

[63] Ibid., p. 447.

[64] Ibid., p. 546.

[65] *Life of Grattan*, v, 552.

[66] Ibid., pp 537, 552.

SELECT BIBLIOGRAPHY

In addition to the primary sources cited in the notes, this biographical essay has drawn on the corpus of historical scholarship relating to Grattan and the issues he addressed during his career. Those listed below will permit the reader to pursue the issues addressed here in fuller detail.

Bartlett, Thomas, *The fall and rise of the Irish nation: the Catholic question, 1690–1829* (Dublin, 1992)

Beckett, J. C., 'Anglo-Irish constitutional relations in the later eighteenth century' in *Confrontations* (London, 1972)

Bolton, G. C., *The passing of the Irish Act of Union* (Oxford, 1966)

Boyce, D. George, *Nationalism in Ireland* (London, 1982)

Butterfield, Herbert, *George III, Lord North and the people* (London, 1949)

Craig, Maurice, *The Volunteer earl* (London, 1948)

Ehrman, John, *The Younger Pitt* (2 vols, London, 1969–83)

Elliott, Marianne, *Wolfe Tone: prophet of Irish independence* (Yale, 1989)

Gwynn, Stephen, *Henry Grattan and his times* (Dublin, 1939)

Johnston, E. M., *Great Britain and Ireland, 1760–1800: a study in political administration* (Edinburgh, 1963)

Jupp, P. J. 'Earl Temple's viceroyalty and the question of renunciation, 1782–3', *Irish Historical Studies*, xvii, 68 (Sept. 1971), pp 499–520

Kelly, James, 'The genesis of Protestant ascendancy' in Gerard O'Brien (ed.), *Parliament, politics and people* (Dublin, 1989)

Kelly, James, *Prelude to union: Anglo-Irish politics in the 1780s* (Cork, 1992)

Lammey, David, 'The growth of the "Patriot opposition" in Ireland during the 1770s', *Parliamentary History*, vii (1988), pp 257–81

Lecky, W. E. H., *A history of Ireland in the eighteenth century* (5 vols, London, 1892)

Lecky, W. E. H., *Leaders of public opinion in Ireland* (2 vols, London, 1903)

Malcomson, A. P. W., *John Foster: the politics of the Anglo-Irish ascendancy* (Oxford, 1978)

McDowell, R. B., *Ireland in the age of imperialism and revolution, 1760–1801* (Oxford, 1979)

Moody, T. W., and Vaughan, W. E., *A new history of Ireland, iv: Eighteenth-century Ireland, 1691–1800* (Oxford, 1986)

O'Brien, Gerard, 'The Grattan mystique', *Eighteenth-Century Ireland*, i (1986), pp 177–94

O'Brien, Gerard, *Anglo-Irish politics in the age of Grattan and Pitt* (Dublin, 1987)

O'Connell, M. R., *Irish politics and social conflict in the age of the American revolution* (Philadelphia, 1965)

O'Connor, T. M., 'The disagreement between Flood and Grattan' in H. A. Cronne *et al.* (eds), *Essays in British and Irish history . . .* (Belfast, 1949)

Smith, E. A., *Whig principles and party politics: Earl Fitzwilliam and the Whig party* (Manchester, 1975)

Smyth, P. D. H., 'The Volunteers and parliament, 1779–84' in Thomas Bartlett and David Hayton (eds), *Penal era and golden age* (Belfast, 1979), pp 113–36

Thorne, R. G. (ed.), *The history of parliament, 1790–1820* (5 vols, London, 1986)

Vaughan, W. E. (ed.), *A new history of Ireland*, v: *Ireland under the union, I: 1800–70* (Oxford, 1989)